KIND PRAISE FOR *THE APRICOT MEMOIRS*

"Women are beginning to speak in so many ways, but one of the most exciting moments for me personally is when they sing in the sound of poetry and creative prose. Tess Guinery's language and form are reminiscent of R. M. Rilke and Nayyirah Waheed, and she is distinguishing herself through a voice that continuously pours contemplation in an unhurried and hopeful stream. *The Apricot Memoirs* as a collection is like a psaltry for the dreamer within us, and it's hard to read these pages without feeling close to the woman herself. Guinery has taken her gaze for design and transformed the seeing eye into the eloquent pen. I'm excited for women everywhere to benefit from a writer who is like the wise older sister we all wished we had. Maybe we still do."

—Teresa Archer, *Darling* magazine

"It is hard not to be immediately drawn into Tess's world—with its ethereal language and heartfelt guidance. We are excited about everything she does, and this work is no exception!"

—Emma Roberts & Karah Preiss, *Belletrist*

"'Within poetry, there is painting, within paintings, there is poetry'—Su Shi (1037–1101). When I came across this quote, Tess Guinery's work immediately came to mind as among those that really embodies the interwoven nature of these artistic forms. She paints with her words and speaks poetry with her paintings. I have found much encouragement from her prose, which have been songs and psalms for my own soul. So much gratitude for the warmth and truth that they hold. Thank you, Tess, for your willingness to share your soul through your poetry and paintings."

—Allison Chan, reader of *The Apricot Memoirs*

THE

APRICOT MEMOIRS

Tess Guinery

Andrews McMeel
PUBLISHING®

Andrews McMeel Publishing
a division of Andrews McMeel Universal
1130 Walnut Street, Kansas City, Missouri 64106

www.andrewsmcmeel.com

21 22 23 24 25 SDB 10 9 8 7 6 5 4 3 2 1

ISBN: 978-1-5248-6472-9

Library of Congress Control Number: 2020948533

Editor: Kevin Kotur
Cover Art and Creative Direction: Tess Guinery
Production Editor: Elizabeth A. Garcia
Production Manager: Carol Coe
Talent Management: Holly Masters

The Apricot Memoirs was originally self-published in 2018 by Morgan Printing, Sydney, Australia, thanks to the management of Holly Masters, the mentorship of Skie Peterson, and editing from Melissa Thielmann.

ATTENTION: SCHOOLS AND BUSINESSES:
Andrews McMeel books are available at quantity discounts with bulk purchase for educational, business, or sales promotional use. For information, please e-mail the Andrews McMeel Publishing Special Sales Department:
specialsales@amuniversal.com.

FSC
www.fsc.org
MIX
Paper from
responsible sources
FSC® C144853

Dedicated to the seekers.

She was created to be sketched on.

Accustomed to tears,
sunlight fade, and whiskey stains—
her corners, curled.

Wildflowers pressed between her textures,
her pages gift
a fragrantly apricot word.

Her pilgrimage:
one set of hands to another,
giving what is needed—
a word in season.

She is a creation.
A song to be shared.
Silent breaths kept for
a quiet place.

Open her with an open heart—
for her story will leave you a gift.
Write it down, but most of all,
let her sentiments
provoke change. . . .

APRICOT MEMOIRS

My soul has been wrestling, a windswept wrestle—she smells like dusk and looks like a sandstorm.

I don't want to slap glitter stickers across a season I'm yet to fully articulate; a season that demands more than my pen knows how. So, for now, here are some excerpts, partial moments that exist somewhere within the story, and it's my hope that one day I may have the wisdom to build words around them.

Words, they come when they do. These memoirs flow in order of their writing, some tucked in spontaneously, having arrived at midnight—an imperfectly beautiful rhythm. Delve into their unexpected crescendos with moments to breathe and moments to move. Chew them in full or savor them slow.

Burrow on through, but only with a perfumed tea resting in one hand (or a whiskey in the other).

When the sabbatical calls,
even if your pockets are empty,
listen to her voice;
she brings all that can't be bought.

THE
APRICOT MEMOIRS

Paint rocks with rainbows,
sketch the female form.
Write words that flow at midnight,
dance till breaking dawn.
Light my walls magenta,
bake a cake and watch it rise.
Open all the windows,
create gifts to say, "Surprise!"
Eat meals by candlelight—
just because—why not?
Sip rouge under moonlight,
Skinny dip, café hop.

Kiss my loves in the morning,
again amid the day.
Sway—upon my to-do list,
know when it's called "a day."

Listen to that still, small voice,
dance unto its sound.
Love this life I've been gifted,
knowing I've been found.

Trusting in the greater plan,
I leave my agenda slow—
holding not a worry,
because He loves me so.

THE
APRICOT MEMOIRS

I took my hair out of its confined topknot
and harsh-hustle demeanor and tied the
ends to the corners of the stars.

THE APRICOT MEMOIRS

Stillness: the fastest train there is—the currency of rest, the pillow where our dream state awakens.

Walk in the rhythm you have been graced
with; rebel against the waves that demand
you—breathe slow.

THE APRICOT MEMOIRS

Smell the peonies with a pocketful of mountaintops, and let not restlessness walk with the silhouettes of slow dances. May slowness catapult you into velvet skies.

Bags beneath the eyes hinder bright horizons, yet sequins under the lashes help one create, unwavering and full of color—

Prayer dust.

THE APRICOT MEMOIRS

I casually ask myself questions to see what returns. That way, the answers can bound toward me without needing to be fully rounded—they twirl and play and even sometimes applaud their own nonsense. I catch them laughing as they hold hands with ideas that terrify my inner politesse. And as they offer their swordplay in teacups and saucers, I take a sip, turn off the night lamp, and fall to sleep.

THE APRICOT MEMOIRS

The bare feet of my pen move across
untouched textures—and words, pouring
like rain, turn unspoken prayers into
castles lit with stars.

Be lovely to those you see undeserving—
oh, the dare in that. Just you wait. Wait till
you see what happens: you'll discover on
the other side.

When we lay down our peace-chasing
rituals—He paints colors all over them,
hangs them on the clothesline to dry,
folds them into tens, multiplies them into
hundreds, and sends them out across
the seven seas like paper airplanes—
meanwhile girding and gifting us with
a peace made of soil and stone—while
our efforts land beautifully in trees and
become mere homes to the birds—

Grace.

APRICOT MEMOIRS

It happened in the darkness of a hotel room that was home for a little while. My romantic heart likens it to that moment when you are laying low under the midnight perfumes without a sound in sight, and something riding on the breeze aligns with everything your thoughts have never been able to speak. Suddenly, the midnight sun rises—nothing is demanding your attention, but simultaneously, all the urgency in the world is storming around you—calling you, prompting you to change it *all*. It's as though your internal and external dialogues become one, while revelations wrapped in fearless change beckon you toward an affectionate ultimatum—

"Tomorrow I'm changing my life."

APRICOT MEMOIRS

As the sun set, it tried to cool the heat we
made, the love we wilded, the hands we
held.

This fierce love
made of sandstorms and stone,
hot to the core,
sweet to the bone—
will always be you.

Our souls burning like embers—
and all the journeys around the sun
will never cool
this love-fire down.

God speaks to us all differently—
that, to me, is the most beautiful thing
I've ever heard.

THE
APRICOT MEMOIRS

If my current ways can no longer carry me, I don't want to row in that boat any longer. I stand face-to-face with dark-yet-kind storm clouds, smiling at me with secrets of splendor; and just like a song, I sing right at them with fierce ocean eyes, asking them to sway toward me—I want the change & the thirst & the mess & the surge & the growth & the freedom & the creativity—I want the alchemy of it all to charge at me like a dance with no shoes.

We were never created for comfy.

THE
APRICOT MEMOIRS

Allow solitude, and choose it from time to time.

I open my heart and breathe in the winds
of change as though my lungs depend
on them.

"I do."
"I do."—

Life's second-greatest alchemy.

THE
APRICOT MEMOIRS

If it's not a poem, quiet thy words—

A rebuttal to gossip.

Forever a sweet seeker, hauling out the beautiful understory in the plainest of narratives—the undertow beneath the waves. I'll forever believe that everything isn't simply two dimensional, but in every moment, a story is being mysteriously orchestrated with purpose by the great hands of our Creator.

THE APRICOT MEMOIRS

My greatest undoing, my brightest
adventure—all five senses sparking to the
music—sweeter than ever before.

The sun—a fragrance like dandelion,
the stars—like fire,
the sand—like clouds,
and the wine—like sweet solace.
Eyes walking asleep, and my mind: a slow
song with an unexpected crescendo.

Nothing can prepare one for such a time
as this.

Let yourself undo, the sooner the
sweeter—

Motherhood.

THE APRICOT MEMOIRS

Anyone can dream in the early morn with a coffee in hand. But when 3:00 p.m. strikes, it's then you have to fight for those sweet sunrise dreams.

Patterns: a rhythmic teacher reminding me of His consistent, persistent love. I connect all the dots amid my messy soul—He, graciously, re-creating me into something irresistible—just like Him. Here I am, in His midst—arms open and unafraid.

Something happened that day at Salvation Mountain: I left a bucketful of tears in the desert, a well to the wildflowers—my lungs, now breathing diamonds.

Our most truthful stance comes easy when the curtains are open, the moon is high, and the morning sun has permission to rise unguarded.

So here I am. It's Friday night, the candles bloom, and tomorrow is spacious in all its beauty. Who cares if the tears fall and the answers are ugly—I dig, I ask, and I let the truth find me. The questions fly freely around the pink walls of our 1960s shack, and I let the returning words banter with themselves, collecting their echoes like glimmering dragonflies—one by one— holding them in a glass jar, and sealing them with a twelve o'clock kiss.

Choose to be a conversationalist—

Intimacy.

Seek springs of life, and always from above—you'll forever know the meaning of ultimate and true love.

She masqueraded around sheepishly, as though she had nothing to say, hiding her most spirited parts in dusty hollows. She stripped off her dignity, leaving it in a puddle by the door. How dare she be "too much"—how dare she . . . be. She kept herself composed, neat and packaged, habitually conditioning herself quiet and as small as can be. Before she knew it, she had become all but shadows—

Once upon a long time ago . . .

THE
APRICOT MEMOIRS

All
unmasking
intimacy
I have ever come to know
has grown
from communion—

Just talk.

If you can celebrate it,
celebrate it!—

Hymn.

Did you choose to see those little love letters? The wistful palms overhead, the cedar stone perfuming the winds with her scent, the prose of life wooing your sweet and pretty soul?

How transformative are words? Shaping the worlds around us, just as water carves homes in rocks. A proverb once did this for me: "Discover beauty in everyone."

Forever defining how I want to live my life—in all matters and things.

APRICOT MEMOIRS

It was as though color walked back into my life, in the form of a 1960s rainbow shack by the sea.

I laugh out loud as I sit barefoot, wrapped in a towel on the lounge room floor. I can hear the ocean. I can smell the salty breeze. I look around and see: blue, yellow, coral, and green—the walls—they're not subtle but loud. It's as if each wall confirms the beautiful story that got me to my now. My internal dialogue rolls over and over with sentimental thank-yous, and then, mid-laugh, I blurt out, "All that, just to get me here?" Then I remember I'm sitting on the floor alone and talking to the heavens—my stubborn nature certainly needed a dangling carrot to get me to this colorful now. And perhaps a pair of birds-eye glasses could have saved me a bucket of tears. But alas, I'm here and I'm having one of those "Ahhh, I get it" moments. I feel a strong sense of peace within this divine encounter, and as I let it settle, I begin to see purpose embedded within every wall of this little rainbow love shack.

THE
APRICOT MEMOIRS

The delivery of gossip never leaves
one enriched, just as the eager ear only
ever walks away burdened with dull
assumptions.

Life is simple:
plant seeds,
water seeds—

Purpose.

THE APRICOT MEMOIRS

Heart breathes, creation.
Mind blooms,
with thoughts strung to the stars.

Voice resounds, with clarity echoing
against the moon.

Feet step in the direction of fierce hope,
watering other flowers and causing them
to grow—

A secure heart.

Plans will change.
That's what makes them plans.

A holiday—never the long-term answer; nor
is shading your hair falu.
Freedom is not reclaimable on a dance floor.
And love cannot be earned.
It is all a matter of the heart; like all things,
an inside job.

I chased peace with my rituals and got nothing but a sack of lack—an unquenchable thirst. But then I sat still, and peace clothed me.

Peace is infinite and beyond understanding, a free gift that dances across our darkest days, when our rituals are too tiring to carry us, and it gifts us anyway.

We are in the pursuit of openness, within
a culture often too busy to deal with the
honesty of hearts: beneath us likely a river
of unshed tears, bottled up, held tight,
storehoused for years as we grit teeth just
"getting it done." It's almost as though we
are discouraged out of our divine state of
creation.

I wonder why that is, when cascading
from that open river is all that is true and
noble and lovely.

Fear takes up residence after sneaking through the back gate. Overstaying its welcome, convincing us to wander into polite submission. If you can pause long enough to see what's going on, you'll discover the seed far before you find yourself living beneath the tree it makes. It takes a willing ear to hear lady wisdom whisper her revelations, so let the maverick in you rise to the occasion, scatter the seeds, and let them fly back into the big, open nothingness from which they came. The sway into freedom will show you how to live (again).

THE
APRICOT MEMOIRS

Chasing the wind, yet still on time—

Creative integrity.

APRICOT MEMOIRS

Be gentle and kind to yourself,
take those scary plunges one syllable at
a time—

Voice.

45

THE
APRICOT MEMOIRS

Whether it be the quiet whispers of the human heart or the vivacious curves of the female form, may we not exploit ourselves—

Deciphering the cyber jungle.

THE
APRICOT MEMOIRS

Where openness is invited,
treasure is found.
I've seen connections birthed in "what-do-
you-dos?" and "where-are-you-froms?"
begin
and
escape
any true sense of intimacy—
chitchats and skimmed sounds
fizzling and leaving you unacquainted
where it counts.
Where openness is invited,
communion is found.

Let those golden words tumble out of your mouth, and when it happens, almost fortuitously, try not to rescue them too quickly—

Vulnerability.

One of the most profound expressions of love: conceiving and nurturing our babes. But equally as powerful during that initial flourish of motherhood: the rebirth of our deepest insecurities—the very ones we have worked so hard to overcome. There is a hefty pull to cover up the feelings of confusion and discomfort, to appease unspoken expectations, and act as though everything is all so *fine*. Truthfully, I have always found that human love is: vulnerable, fragile, ugly, beautiful—and entirely worth it—

Motherhood.

THE APRICOT MEMOIRS

Reaching for a pen—
oh, the words that have
whirled,
pooled,
and slipped down the drain
while washing my hair.

THE APRICOT MEMOIRS

Words before flowers—always.

THE APRICOT MEMOIRS

Starts with a bloom—hearts dancing,
boom boom
beating like a drum,
sipping rouge and rum
hearts on fire
petals like rain
you kiss me under storm clouds
the roses are to blame.

Here's to facing fears—again. Doing it with style, keeping it casual while I sit mid-flight, enjoying a calming cider, laughing anxiously through the turbulence—

Overcoming.

Life's biggest blunder: captaining our own soul.

This "greater being" you speak of, the one that's been epitomized into mere haze, trees, and magic—

He, my love, is the meaning of life.

Romance isn't something that magically falls upon some and flies over others—it's a choice.

Your sweet, loving choice.

Slowly I learned, and slowly I became enamored by the beat of slow.

Teach my soul rest: the greatest wrestle of my sweet little life.

THE
APRICOT MEMOIRS

"Why am I so busy?"

It took thirty-three years of journeying
around the golden circle before I was
ready to honestly climb this question.
I knew that the answer, in its quick and
quiet breath, would hold both my great
unraveling, and my rebuilding.

THE APRICOT MEMOIRS

Your ultimate love has run me out of my ultimate dreams.

THE APRICOT MEMOIRS

I'm clumsy, crazy & about you.

THE
APRICOT MEMOIRS

All that is golden like an apricot, likely has
a bed of prayer beneath it.

APRICOT MEMOIRS

Notice where you are when you unfold,
notice where you are when you have breath.

As dusk illuminates the coral arches of the place we call home, peace fills our lungs with a knowing—it breathes a slow-revealing map, drawing our hearts toward mysteries and unknown landscapes. All is well, even in the waiting. Together we prayed for the "suddenlies" and the dreaming has enveloped our life (chasing us free).

Fill your well with the intangible; listen
to the sounds that are a decibel below
a whisper—

Thrum.

There is no point dancing if your intuition is telling you that now is a time to rest. Just like there's no point in resting if momentum is circling you like a beautiful hurricane.

So, what is your now?—

Seasons.

Why must we insist people do as they're told rather than teaching them to trust their God-given instincts and inclinations?

THE APRICOT MEMOIRS

Some days I dance, prance, and finesse
the gifts of my golden hands like a rogue
exhibitionist. My ways grow tiresome,
as the glitter turns to dust, and I catch a
squinted glimpse—yet again—of the One
who created time, beyond time, and out of
time & I hear the whisper loudly—

"Time belongs to me; go to sleep!"

THE
APRICOT MEMOIRS

The currency of Heaven is upside down, inside out, reversed, shaken, fizzed up, and stirred. Inappropriately overflowing, rebelliously loving, out of our rhythm and into its own. Mysteriously boundless, surprisingly wholehearted, perfectly uncalculated, and wrapped in fabric made from silk and stars. In its ways— anarchic, yet ordered and aligned with raw and solid gold. Swaying—hair out and laughing, holding hands with Earth's muddy paws—barefooted and dancing as though the Earth were a stage to make sandstorms for beauty's sake.

When was the last time you told yourself
that you are a good mumma—that the
nourishment and nurture you provide is
abundant and plentiful as it shapes a little
learning life into a walking, beating love
heart?

Let your heart feel risk; keep it wild.

★

Close your eyes—I have more to show you.

My insides—forever wrestling with the rhythms of fast and slow. I favor them equally.

In a beautiful world that has come to hooray the hustle, I find my sweet-loving soul rebelliously dancing to the contrary. For this season, busy has no place—busy cannot lasso my time. It is down by the river, sunbathing on silky rocks.

I'm choosing an agendaless season where hurry doesn't live but flowers do grow.

THE APRICOT MEMOIRS

Meet your own blindness
and command that it would see;
hold this fire, humbly,
and ask how you should pray.

I look back over my shoulder and see, clear in view, a series of intentional decisions made under the aubade of surrender with gritted teeth and messy hair. And in front of me, I see beauty encompassing my life.

How do you recognize the muse?

She's often nonchalant and barefoot beneath a tree, reading her book—only caring to be found by those daring enough to seek her out.

Whenever I have seen momentum in my life, there has always been a choice to yield first.

Unity materializes into flow.
Flow materializes into love.
And love
completes.
It completes all.

Speak all kinds of beautiful and watch your world change—words are powerful enough to make worlds.

THE
APRICOT MEMOIRS

Notebook on nightstand—lady wisdom,
she insists on intruding inconveniently—

A ready heart.

In love. Enlightened. My heart unashamedly
sewn to my outside pocket, I let these truths
seep into my skin, running over and over
on paths and hills and roads before me.
I'm singing with the flowers, dancing with
the desert, roaring with the mountains, and
swimming in the storms. Internal prayers
echoing boldly, heart crying, countenance
grounded, head above the clouds, and
gemstones resting on my ankles. Oh, what
love can do, to a heart that truly chooses Him.

Dance does things
that sometimes words can't.

Anyone can love the loveable.
But love is tested on the other side of
irritation:
an overstayed welcome,
opposite sways,
misunderstandings,
different ways.
If we can allow ourselves to sit
on open hillsides,
this is where we'll find communion—
love ain't pretty—it's messy & confronting
& challenging & uncomfortable & an
in-your-face kind of *beautiful*!
Fight for the messy; love lives beneath it.

Is it a thing to be an introverted expressionist?

There's art in my hair,
poetry beneath my shoes,
ornaments in the sky, and
pink lavender in the moon.

THE APRICOT MEMOIRS

Although many bear witness to your joy,
few will know the battles you fight to keep it.

THE APRICOT MEMOIRS

My pen pursues a zephyr holding words, free-falling with ink while overcoming the blankness. Words that pave paths to my "aha" moments—or to the beginnings of some. Wrapping up, summing together, tying a knot, leading me home—

Paper revelations.

Comfort with the unknown: the silver
lining of faith.

THE APRICOT MEMOIRS

Here's to the seekers, the delvers,
the color chasers, and ocean shakers,
salt of the earth, sweet child of the sun.

Unravel your heart—over and over
and over some more.

Refuse comfy,
let your fire burn.
Choose the way of conversation,
and leave no rock unturned.

Ask a zillion questions,
and then ask again, "Why?"
May you never silence internal directives,
or bottle up a cry.

You, my dear, are full of wonder,
made for what's in store,
flowers paving paths of purpose,
heart beating, growing more.

Pick up your tambourine,
grace this brand new day.
Less comfort, more life—
Get up, get on your way.

THE
APRICOT MEMOIRS

I'll tell you a secret I discovered awhile
back: God isn't mean. He smiles & creates
& delights over us with playful songs.

And the rain fell heavy,
carrying hope in its hands.

THE APRICOT MEMOIRS

I'd rather poetry in my hair
and paint beneath my feet
than caviar on the table
and jewels forever to keep.

(The miracle remains) I can actually say,
for a season of my life, I painted rainbows
for a living—rainbows paid my bills while
paint filled my soul.

Yes, wisdom is a must, when unraveling in spaces and places with vulnerability and our art. But I'll call it a disloyalty to our nature, if we wait until it's safe to reveal our hearts.

What a catastrophe, if we never allow our hearts to explore risk.

Leave him a love note—there is wild in
the simple.

THE APRICOT MEMOIRS

One day he'll tell me to gather my things.
Without a question in sight, my soul will
sing "hallelujah." It will be at dusk, my
imagination remembers it so. And we
will get wildly excited for all the unknown
reasons. I'll water the plants, turn off
the salt lamps, and watch them melt. I'll
notice how happy I was here and pack
everything precious into a bag or two. My
days of buying wooden bowls and rattan
baskets will be mere "remember the days."
I'll smile at the waiting and won't even ask
why we are leaving—because this drifter's
heart has known, under her composed
demeanor, all her pretty life.

I love being a daughter of the Heavens. To some, narrow—but to me, it's that expansive kind of liberation we all dream about—beyond burn your bra, speak your mind, do what you want—it's a life-breathed unchaining, free-falling with wings. It whispers honeyed melodies that have my heart somersaulting with expectation. It says, "Your life has soul!"—

I have found purpose, and I'm never letting it go.

The unquenchable thirst that shadows busy feet cannot be relieved by the tireless motions of self—only the opposite. The currency of Heaven is upside down, and I love all of its cheeky irony.

I'm a vessel—

Humility.

In a time such as now, creativity will speak the unspeakable—cutting through opinions, bringing rest, ushering unity.

The muse: a delightful, playful, duty-less
mystery—she leads us fearlessly into wide
and open spaces.

THE
APRICOT MEMOIRS

When imagination returns,
it means we are back in our body.

Tears prepare the clay our future feet
will walk.

THE APRICOT MEMOIRS

If I choose to always grow,
maybe she will bloom like a wildflower.
If I make art from my everyday,
she too will fill her days with color.
If I let my tears fall always when they need,
perhaps she'll water the earth with an open heart.
If I'm clumsy-crazy and all about her dad,
a beautiful, crazy love is what her heart will search for.
If I let him forever romance me in the wake of day,
she will never know less.
If I say "I'm sorry," even when it's hard,
maybe she'll be quick to forgive others.
If I choose to speak life in vibrant and rich colors,
beige words won't settle in her heart.
If I leave pretty love notes, handwritten on every wall,
affirmations will hold the depth of her soul.
If I choose the uncomfy and forever shake up my ways,
maybe she too will stand to live bold and brave.
If I take time to be alone and practice dreaming,
she'll learn solitude is important, a golden gift to seek.
If I look in the mirror and speak kind and gentle words,
she too will forever know her worth.
If I fill our house with flowers, music, and sweet, loving scents,
maybe the silhouette of home will always be warmth.
If our front door is always open to those who are in need,
she'll learn the golden purpose of life.
If I pray out loud and have real conversations with God,
maybe she'll move mountains with her voice.

If I tell her I love her a million times a day,
maybe, just maybe, she'll learn:
even in my flaws,
my lack,
and my mistakes,
I gave her my entire heart—

My motherhood monologue.

What we say
is how we'll sway.

Not to be confined to the paintbrush but released and eaten whole in the living, the doing, the talking, the being—

Creativity.

APRICOT MEMOIRS

When we are dreaming, creating, and reckoning with greater horizons, we have less time to stop and talk about others (in that dull kind of way). Rather, we find ourselves talking in beautiful arrays of color, building paths of unity—

Prolific conversation.

Sometimes we are given the opportunity to make a brave choice. A choice to surrender the things that have been great, in exchange for greater. It's here a soulful, lively, *boom-boom*, heart-out-of-chest, tears-on-cheeks "I'm alive" kind of passion lives. It lives just around the corner from surrender's bend.

It's 5:05 a.m. She's jumped out of bed again, telling me there's a monkey on the back of the door. She's right! Those towels really do silhouette a monkey—

Imagination.

Internal fibs can't defeat you when you're busy marching the skies.

If you see something beautiful in someone,
tell them.

THE
APRICOT MEMOIRS

Sharing nostalgia: life's sweetest cup of tea.

You'll never know what people truly think
of you—assume it's lovely.

Over time, tender gestures become romantic culture.

THE
APRICOT MEMOIRS

A triumphant manifesto of creativity is about to make its home on planet Earth. Will you pioneer or wait for the rain to fall?

THE
APRICOT MEMOIRS

We were created by a Creator—create.

THE APRICOT MEMOIRS

What are you dreaming about
What makes your flower-heart bleed
How do you like your coffee (or tea)
And did you exhale large in the ocean breeze?

Did you say that thing your heart needed
What song best describes your now
What wakes you up at midnight to pray
Did you turn up the music and sing too loud?

Did you take the day-nap you needed
And what pretty things do you see
What miracle happened at lunchtime
Did you take time to sit still and just be?

What risks are you taking
What changes are you making
Is your heart growing
What seeds are you sowing?

What awakens your heart
What makes it burn
What makes you cry
Or your stomach dance and turn?

Who do you love
And why is it so
Where could you live
How far would you go?

Did you open imagination's door
Did you make some time to sway
Did you hug somebody, darling—
Please tell me about your pretty day.

THE
APRICOT MEMOIRS

I'm reading books like I'm alive at midnight, sipping ruby-flavored whiskey— sweetly wild, fiercely frolicsome—

Moonlight oil.

The song of freedom, to some, is fear in color.

THE
APRICOT MEMOIRS

Leave a place in love; arrive on purpose.

Beauty can be squeezed out of rocks—

Improvisation.

Your soul will find truth in essence, not trends.

The laughers dream & the dreamers laugh most.

We can never be totally, fully, and colorfully
free until we have forgiven.

APRICOT MEMOIRS

Fortresses built carelessly with sticks, mortar, and bitterness will fall away just like the dust on moth wings in the faintest breath of wind.

When your insides feel like they could explode with an eternal "Yes!!!!!!!!!!!!!"—

Sipping with kindred.

The moment we define ourselves by our doings, we have lost our way.

THE
APRICOT MEMOIRS

I am not afraid to say I am beautiful. I have sifted meticulously through the salt mines, and my head rests—even in the residue, it rests.

A love that was not afraid to extravagantly
adore me, before I was ready—

The Good News.

I'm showing up, world.
In all my failings and in all my beauty,
I am showing up—

Wholly.

APRICOT MEMOIRS

When a season of waiting is confusingly
beautiful, drink the sunrise for breakfast
and kiss the balmy palms at night—

Making the most of everything.

THE APRICOT MEMOIRS

Since my heart found home,
seeking it here has become void.

The sound of a squawking bird
at 5:30 a.m.—

Flattery.

The secret place: a glass of forever.

My imagination: where I commune with
the most real breath I know.

He did just as my heart needed that day:
he bought me flowers, told me I was crazy,
but said he loved me anyway.

THE APRICOT MEMOIRS

My internal revolution was less about
shadowing and more about rebelliously
finding my way; a way that was colorfully
contrary to what I once called freedom.

Night is Heaven's gift—cooling the heat
of the day with a kiss, a trinket of plum,
and a side of sweet—

It's here I feel most human.

When the heart's reluctant, stop and ask
it why.

When I say I need time alone, what I really mean is: I want to move all the furniture around and then move it all back. I want to paint something and leave the brushes to bristle all because I decided to go wash my hair. I'll forget to take my multi-vs—I was busy trying on dresses. Suddenly, I'll move every plant to the tiles in the sunroom, just to water them. The plants will make like a jungle at the front door because there was that book I once read, explaining the cycle of butterflies, so I'll rummage around for it, but in my hunt, I'll find old photos—sleeping in nostalgia for what feels like ten minutes. Suddenly it's dusk. Dinner will be the last thing on my mind. I'll likely throw a handful of vegetables into some batter and, amid the kitchen mess, I'll pour some Spanish wine while closing my eyes at the same time. I'll light some candles, open all the windows, change the sheets, and fall asleep early because nothing excites me more.

When I say I need time alone, this is really what I mean.

Maybe we aren't actually afraid anymore—maybe we only feel an obligation to our fears?

I thought studying the Creator was the way to meet Him. I found Him when I finally allowed my imagination to dance with His.

THE
APRICOT MEMOIRS

There is a gentle rhythm when walking
in step with one another, learning
the nuances of unfamiliar voices—
simply nesting together sans words and
expectations. Eager to come together and
okay to be apart.

Naysayers, gloom swayers: they—just beautiful souls with clipped wings and a sleepy dreamer's heart.

Vulnerability: the moment our true humanity is revealed and our self-taught defenses, diminished.

THE
APRICOT MEMOIRS

I
Can
Make
The
World
Beautiful—
Says the large heart.

Judgment: A symptom of the heart that has forgotten to choose love—in essence, the heart that has narrowed.

THE
APRICOT MEMOIRS

He—a balmy night.
She—a radical morning—

An extreme dyad.

THE
APRICOT MEMOIRS

Secret landmarks of the heart: the internal map of growth.

THE
APRICOT MEMOIRS

You've taught me how little I know
and how hugely the heart can love—
motherhood.

THE
APRICOT MEMOIRS

Speak in golden beams with the women of your walk, and hold those harvest words, letting kindness lead your talk.

Honor your hunches, dance/learn/grow
with the punches.

We are praying when we laugh.

Prayer transcends the ritual of kneeling knees. It's a wild and creative communion, lying within the sigh, the shout, the tears, the dance—a talkative electricity alive in, and through, our being.

Hints and prompts followed by guesses and grace—

Faith.

You can't be misunderstood when you pray.

Surrender feels like clean air in the lungs.

THE APRICOT MEMOIRS

Sometimes you are just simmering for a season called "next"—

Waiting well.

<small>THE</small> APRICOT MEMOIRS

Surrender can be held.

APRICOT MEMOIRS

Every time the phone rang, she thought it
to be good news—

Heart of an optimist.

Living in fear and calling it life—

My greatest fear.

THE APRICOT MEMOIRS

The lull after surrender was beige, though
I expected it rainbow. The risk was in
the letting go and my heart was alive in
rebellion. In the colorless aftermath, I dug
in the ruins for signs of the great. I looked
for stones, pebbles even—collecting
them into my back pocket, hoping they'd
grow into wildflowers. You can't gray
this optimist's heart. I'd sleep at midday
(I only sleep in the day when my heart
becomes beige), waiting, hoping. My
surroundings—beige. But with every call,
a chance for greatness. With every turn, a
chance for a new path—

I will wait for your promise. I know it's
coming. . . .

So for now, I'll paint rainbows.

THE
APRICOT MEMOIRS

I am redeeming,
holding,
reclaiming,
God's handmade gifts to Earth,
as though they were made with me
in mind—the moon, the stars, the scents,
the stones.

I am flying high above
what mortal hands have made,
frozen from what they truly are—

Awe-inspiring gifts made by the hands
of a golden Creator.

I'm building my life on the World's Greatest Mystery—the only sure thing I know.

THE
APRICOT MEMOIRS

Words received in pink when they were
spoken in fuchsia—

Miscommunication.

THE
APRICOT MEMOIRS

Life, you big, delicious gift.
In one hand, you offer us beauty,
and in the other—
more often than we'd hope—
shadows.

But it's here,
in this place,
the eyes begin to see,
the ears begin to hear,
and the art is made.

THE
APRICOT MEMOIRS

Commune with the still, small voice—often.

Everyday life: a resounding prayer.

THE APRICOT MEMOIRS

When I finally dropped my handmade dress, I was overwhelmed by my nakedness. Social awkwardness became my sunlight stance. My hunt to hide, laid to rest in the gift of nighttime. With regrets of my wish for wholeheartedness—a tenacity for truth (like a motor roaring underneath my skin)—I'd count sunsets and wish to be like the sanguines. Here I am, forever obliging to the search, the climb, the undertows. If only I could turn this humming off, I would.

I pray you find communion, where things get beautifully impolite.

THE
APRICOT MEMOIRS

Open all the windows,
the doors and the curtains,
Welcome the seemingly ordinary,
allow it to move you.

I have officially resigned to the itinerary
for my life—

The Greater Plan.

Let your bright eyes be held by the sun—
you'll see the very best light, in everyone.

THE
APRICOT MEMOIRS

A facade can't stick
when your arms are in the air,
shake them around
with luminous color and flare!

Freedom is a rainbow,
a staircase to a door,
palm trees making archways,
prompting hearts to grow some more.

Choose to dance with fervor,
dare not to stay the same,
know that there is so much more:
your heart is known by name.

Sometimes—it's only one hair wash away in the shower while praying.

And other times—it's 167 hair washes away, all until one day, mid-rinse, you forget what you have been praying for—

Forgiveness.

May our choices be made not on the
back of fads but set on fire in the grit and
beauty of solemn soil.

Don't think that everything you think is a thought is true.

THE APRICOT MEMOIRS

We find our voice when we lend our ears
to the voice of the Creator.

Imagine how high you could fly
if you knew that you belonged.

THE
APRICOT MEMOIRS

Let the walls of your home
hear poems about others.

Speak to others as though they are already
on their mountaintop.

APRICOT MEMOIRS

5:21 a.m. Sunrise.
My words, traveling safely.
I wanted you to be real, and my faith told
me you were—my head, loud with hope.

One hour later. Faith ruled over my head.
You are, in fact, real! Two little lines
confirming it was you all along—the fourth
and fifth presence that day, on the living
room floor, while the three of us laughed
as we put our hands to a jigsaw.

I never thought I'd be ready for you, and
here I am—ready for two!

A walk through rocky provinces has
prepared the earth within me. And now,
I'm counting down the days while I secretly
smile—you are our beautiful secrets, for
now.

A gift,
a double blessing,
we welcome you, even before you are here.
We love you already, our sunrise news—

Unknown desires (buried in the heart).

Risking
It
All—

Surrender.

The green-eyed monster only exists when you forget your birthright—when you turn a blind eye to the truth that God has beautiful plans for you too!

APRICOT MEMOIRS

The napkins laid witness
while the ears of flowers listened, eager,
and sounds tumbled into open
wine glasses.
It's here I breathe easy,
in spaces and places where dreams
fall out,
with no need to rescue them,
because maybe, why not?

Too big? Too grand?
Absolutely never.
It's easy to stay hidden in the darkness.
Even fools, who choose the flowers over
and over, know that.
And in these spaces and places,
where dreams are held by the light,
others believe with you (and for you).
I'll never unsee
the miracle in this.

THE APRICOT MEMOIRS

Peace is wholeness. And wholeness—quietude.

THE APRICOT MEMOIRS

Something I'm made of wants to tell a story.
There are words in us,
our body carrying them.
Verses wrapped in paragraphs,
essays wrapped in paper—
lining soft walls within us.
I want to listen,
I want to tell.
There is beauty here,
there is beauty here.

THE
APRICOT MEMOIRS

It's okay to be hidden for a season.

The joy in giving will forever outweigh the
gift in receiving—there's a dare in that!

THE APRICOT MEMOIRS

You get to choose what you choose to see.

When a soul carries unforgiveness, it judges.
When a soul is surrendered, it creates.

THE APRICOT MEMOIRS

How many ways can we sing "I love you!"?—

Eternally.

THE
APRICOT MEMOIRS

I picture prayers to be much like wind:
words carried by breaths, circling and
giving momentum to sounds of hope.

THE
APRICOT MEMOIRS

If flowers could speak,
it would sound like them.
Hands—
open,
giving,
holding,
loving.
It's joy you'll find,
when we have sought and found how to
serve—
cheerfully, wholeheartedly, eternally.

You don't need all the things you think you need to do all the things you feel called to do. You have all you need right now, right here—now go make life beautiful!

Surrender pays with a wholeness the world
certainly can't pay you in.

You've given me a pen; I'll forever write
for You—

A vessel.

THE
APRICOT MEMOIRS

I feast and festoon with fireballs deep
within my belly; I commune with an
inspired breath—ancient words—as
though they were a newfound friend. I
digest truth with slow, savored sips, and my
heart rolls tipsy, my eyes silken solid. Later,
the words reveal paths to unexpected
parley with power to open minds—

The Greatest Story Ever Told.

Living in the space of "needing more stuff" means my heart is sipping from the wrong springs.

THE

APRICOT MEMOIRS

Want to know what will rob your life and
tie your dreams into a neat, safe little
parcel?

Abandoning yourself to lifeless banter:
"When I finally get . . ."
"Once I've bought . . ."
"Once we've saved . . ."
Boring, wearisome words.

Waiting for better days
will rob your better days
called "now."

Old worlds are not the only places miracles are found.

THE
APRICOT MEMOIRS

Familiar songs,
newfound words,
breeze in my sleeves,
flying with the birds.

THE APRICOT MEMOIRS

You are loved.
You are beloved.

Some words are best left
swallowed by the light.

Life should be lived with a spirit of adventure, loads of good conversation, and a heart ready to celebrate others. Love your lover, make love under the stars, let your heart feel risk, keep it wild. Follow spontaneity's lead, keep things fresh, and say "I love you" a million times a day. Share a meal and some rouge with your tribe. Don't be tightfisted with what's in your hands—be generous! Generous with: your words, your creativity, and your love. Live large, and heed to your convictions. Don't let the sun set upon anger, and be bold even when you feel like retreating to your safe little cave. Most importantly, have faith, and love God with all your heart, mind, and soul.

I say again: I'm barely able to articulate the seasons past—a season that demands more than my pen, yet knows how. It's my hope that one day I may have the wisdom to build words around these apricot pieces, and maybe they too will become a book.

I am thankful for the call to yield and all that it teaches. The winds of change— they came and, ever so subtly, beckoned. They called me into a sandstorm.

GRATITUDES

Caleb Guinery, the love of my life and holder of dreams, your love for me and faith in God has awoken my eyes to the zillion miracles that happen simply every day—I love you; I love us. My little loves Peaches Wilde, Hopps Golden, and Junee Moon: my muses, because of you, life is beautiful! I love being your mumma.

A very big and special thank-you to Holly Masters, Tony Masters, Morgan Printing, Skie Peterson, Melissa Theilmann, Ryan Perno, and Kaylene Langford—without you, these pages would not exist. I could never conjure enough words or gestures to truly thank you for the love you have sown and poured into this creation (and me). I love you forever.

I want to take a special moment to honor all the behind-the-scenes hands & hearts that have worked in many different capacities on the early and ongoing processes of this book—enabling her pages to materialize from dream state to published form. Mum and Dad, Mumma and Pappa Guinery, Nedra Springer, Hello Hello Studio, Annette Kelsey, Sharee Gray, Bonnie Gray, Selene Sheerin, Teresa Archer, Amanda Jones, Sarah Quinn, Cassia and Garren Walton, Jenny Webb, Matt Webb, Lisa Byers, Ilsa Wynne-Hoelscher, Alex Carlyle, Dan and Hannah Gorry, and Rachael Valentine.

Thank you to Kevin Kotur and Andrews McMeel Publishing for welcoming me into your family of beautiful literature—I'm so grateful for your creativity and how you nurture the artist—thank you for taking these books into new spaces and faraway places (with such love and care).

Thank you to the plethora of generous family and friendships that surround my world (near and far) that have cheered me on, hemmed me in, met me in the eye of life's storms, packed books, offered advice, and clinked glasses with me when life has called for it—I feel blessed and humbled by you (you know who you are)—and I love you!

A massive thank-you to YOU (the reader), the original catalysts aka the Kickstarter backers who set these pages on their way. You have shown up (again & again) with your love, and it's overwhelmingly beautiful!

Sincere songs of gratitude to my Lord and Creator—what a privilege it is to be a vessel and create (because you first created me).

ABOUT THE AUTHOR

Tess Guinery is a dancer by upbringing, a designer by trade, and an artist by calling. After graduating from the Karl von Busse Institute of Design in Australia, she started her own freelance business, soon establishing herself as a sought-after creator with design work bursting at the seams. After seven fond years in the design industry, Tess intuitively pressed pause to take a sabbatical—its intention, to explore her inner artist. This purposeful time led to the making of her tangible art piece *The Apricot Memoirs*. These days, Tess is traveling abroad, calling many places home (for a while) with her stuntman husband and their three spirited daughters.